W9-BLS-868

John F. Kennedy

John F. Kennedy

Kieran Doherty

AMERICA'S 35TH PRESIDENT

Children's Press®
A Division of Scholastic Inc.
New York / Toronto / London / Auckland / Sydney
Mexico City / New Delhi / Hong Kong
Danbury, Connecticut

Library of Congress Cataloging-in-Publication Data

Doherty, Kieran, 1945–
    John F. Kennedy / Kieran Doherty.
      p. cm. — (Encyclopedia of presidents. Second series)
Includes bibliographical references and index.
  ISBN 0-516-22976-1
  1. Kennedy, John F. (John Fitzgerald), 1917–1963—Juvenile literature. 2.
Presidents—United States—Biography—Juvenile literature. 3. United States—
Politics and government—1961–1963—Juvenile literature. I. Title. II.
Encyclopedia of presidents (2003)
E842.Z9D69 2005
973.922'092—dc22   2004019421

CHILDREN'S PRESS and associated logos are trademarks and or registered
trademarks of Scholastic Library Publishing. SCHOLASTIC and associated
logos are trademarks and or registered trademarks of Scholastic Inc.
1 2 3 4 5 6 7 8 9 10 R 14 13 12 11 10 09 08 07 06 05

Contents

Chapter 1

Sudden Ending ————————————

On November 22, 1963, President John Fitzgerald Kennedy and his wife, Jacqueline, were in Dallas, Texas. It was a cool, sunny day when *Air Force One*, the presidential plane, landed at Love Field, just outside the city. The young president—he was just 46 years old—smiled and waved as a motorcade carried him and his wife into downtown Dallas. His wife, dressed in a bright pink suit and matching hat, sat by his side, waving at the crowds that lined the streets.

As the presidential motorcade made its way into the city, an unstable and unhappy man named Lee Harvey Oswald waited. Oswald was an ex-marine. He once lived as an exile in the Soviet Union, and he was angry about U.S. government policies. On this November day he was determined to take action. He crouched at an open window on the sixth floor of a warehouse in downtown Dallas. He was holding a high-powered rifle.

President Kennedy and his wife, Jacqueline, arrive in Dallas, Texas, on November 22, 1963. Only hours later, Kennedy was shot and killed while riding in a motorcade.

As the motorcade passed the warehouse, the president turned to wave to the crowd. Oswald peered through the telescopic sight of his rifle. He sighted on the president's head. He fired one shot, then a second, and then a third.

One bullet smashed through President Kennedy's neck and slammed into Texas governor John Connally, who was sitting in the front seat. Kennedy slumped forward and to the side toward his wife. A second bullet hit the president in the back of his head. The third bullet apparently flew wide of its target.

John F. Kennedy, the 35th President of the United States, was mortally wounded. He died soon afterward in a nearby hospital. He had served just over a thousand days as president. Yet Kennedy's brief term left an indelible mark on the United States and on the presidency.

Family and Childhood

John Fitzgerald Kennedy was born on May 29, 1917, in Brookline, Massachusetts, a suburb of Boston. He was the descendant of Irish families who immigrated to the Boston area in the mid-1800s, when Ireland was ravaged by a great famine. His paternal grandfather, Patrick Kennedy, started as a saloon keeper and became one of the most powerful politicians in Boston. His father, Joseph Patrick Kennedy, graduated from Harvard College and became rich as a banker and businessman. Kennedy's mother, Rose Fitzgerald Kennedy, also came from a political family. She was the daughter of John Francis Fitzgerald, a popular mayor of Boston and U.S. congressman, who was known as "Honey Fitz."

John, always called Jack by his family and friends, was the second of nine children born to Joe Kennedy and his wife, Rose. He had an older brother, Joseph Kennedy Jr., called Joe. His younger brothers, Robert (Bobby) and Edward (Ted),

The Kennedy home in Brookline, Massachusetts, where John F. Kennedy was born in 1917. It is now a national historic site.

The Potato Famine

In the early 1800s, most of the people of Ireland depended on the humble potato for food. Beginning in 1845, a disease struck the potato crop, turning the potatoes black and making them inedible. As the crops failed, terrible famine struck the land. The British, who governed Ireland at that time, were unable to provide relief, and in a few years, Ireland's population declined by about 2 million. It is estimated that nearly a million Irish men, women, and children died of starvation and disease. Many others, including John Kennedy's ancestors, left Ireland to settle in Britain and North America.

★ ★ ☆

later had political careers of their own. His sisters, all younger, were Rosemary, Kathleen, Eunice, Patricia, and Jean. When Jack was born, the family was already prosperous. By the time he was a teenager, the Kennedys were very rich. Rose Kennedy always had nannies and maids to help care for the children.

Jack grew up in Brookline, first in the comfortable house where he was born, and later in a much larger home. Then, in 1927, when Jack was ten years old, the family moved to Riverdale, a fashionable and prosperous neighborhood in New York City.

Later in his life, Jack Kennedy said the only thing that bothered him as a child was his constant competition with his older brother, Joe. The two brothers wrestled and ran races and tried to outdo each other in everything. Their father

Rose Kennedy, at left, with her five children in 1922: Eunice, Kathleen, Rosemary (sitting on the ground), John, and Joseph Jr. Four more children were born later—Patricia, Robert, Jean, and Edward.

A Plea for Money

Though the Kennedy family was wealthy, Joseph Kennedy did not believe in giving his children large sums of money. When Jack was ten years old, he received an allowance of 40¢ a week. After the family moved to Riverdale, he decided he needed more. He wrote a letter to his father. His small allowance had been enough to buy the "playthings of childhood," he wrote. Now, though, he had become a "Scout" and he needed "to buy canteens, haversacks, things that will last for years." His letter persuaded his millionaire father to raise his allowance to a whopping 70¢ a week.

☆ ★ ☆

encouraged this competition. He always challenged his children, the girls as well as the boys, to be first in everything. If Jack and the others did not try to win every contest, their father would grow angry.

Rose Fitzgerald Kennedy never showed much affection to her children. Although she loved them dearly, she seemed distant and aloof. Jack was hurt by this lack of affection. "My mother never hugged me," he told a friend late in his life. "Never!"

School Days

Jack Kennedy began his formal education at a public school just a few blocks from his family's home in Brookline. Two years later, he and his brother Joe attended the Dexter School, a private boys' school nearby. Most Dexter students were the sons of Boston's wealthy (and mostly Protestant) families. Roman Catholic students like the Kennedys were rare. The other boys taunted Joe and Jack because of their religion, and they were forced to fight back. Jack, younger and smaller than Joe, was their main target.

After the family moved to Riverdale, Jack enrolled in Riverdale Country School, a private academy. At Riverdale, Jack was not a very good student, though he loved reading and history. In 1930, when Jack was 13, he left home to attend the Canterbury School, a boarding school in western Connecticut. The next year, he transferred to the Choate School, also in Connecticut, one of the nation's most famous prep schools.

When Jack arrived at Choate, his brother Joe had already been there for two years. Joe was, in the words of Choate's headmaster (principal), "one of the 'big boys' of the school." He was on the varsity basketball team and was one of the school's most admired students. Jack wanted desperately to be as good as his older brother at sports and at everything else, but he could not compete. Tall and thin, he was not physically fit enough to make any varsity team. Though he was bright and well read, he simply did not apply himself to his schoolwork. As a result, his grades were not as good as his brother's.

Jack Kennedy (right) and three of his friends at Choate School show off their sporty clothes and smart attitudes.

Jack might have done better in school had he not been sick as often as he was. Even as a baby, he had health problems. At the Canterbury School, he often complained of tiredness. He had many colds and blurred vision. At Choate he suffered from a variety of stomach and intestinal complaints. Even when he was not sick in bed, he was rarely completely healthy.

Joe Kennedy graduated from Choate in 1933. For his last two years, Jack didn't have to compete with his older brother. This didn't improve his study habits, and he graduated in 1935, ranked 64th in a class of 112. He did blossom into an active and popular student, however. In his final term, his classmates voted him "most likely to succeed."

Harvard

Jack's family expected him to enroll at Harvard College when he graduated from Choate, but Jack had other plans. Joe was already at Harvard, and Jack didn't want to compete with his older brother once again. He insisted on enrolling at Princeton, another of the exclusive Ivy League colleges. Soon after he arrived on the Princeton campus, however, he fell ill with jaundice (an inflammation of the liver). He was forced to withdraw from school and spent several months at home recuperating. By the fall of 1936, he was well again, and this time he gave in to family pressure. At the age of 19, he enrolled at Harvard.

As a freshman, Jack Kennedy was much more interested in girls, sports, and good times than in studying. He barely scraped by in class. Eventually, while practicing for a football game, he suffered a serious back injury. It would cause him problems for the rest of his life.

The summer after his freshman year, Jack took a trip to Europe. He visited Italy, which was then ruled by the dictator Benito Mussolini, and Germany, where Adolf Hitler and his Nazi party governed with an iron hand. Jack's experiences in these two dictatorships made him interested in politics as he'd never been before.

That fall, President Franklin D. Roosevelt appointed Jack's father, Joseph Kennedy Sr., U.S. ambassador to the United Kingdom (Great Britain). The Kennedy family moved to London, while Jack remained at Harvard, but his father's new position further stirred Jack's interest in politics and world affairs. In 1939, he visited Europe once again. This time, through his father's connections, he was able to talk with leading politicians and diplomats. Germany had taken control of Austria and Czechoslovakia and was threatening to invade other neighboring countries. In Britain and the United States, political leaders were discussing how to deal with Germany's threats.

On September 1, 1939, German armies invaded Poland. Within days, Britain and France declared war against Germany, beginning World War II. Jack returned to Harvard, where he wrote his senior thesis (research paper) about why

Ambassador Joseph Kennedy Sr. (center) with his oldest sons Joe Jr. (left) and Jack (right).

the British government was unprepared for the onset of the war. His thesis was published in 1940 under the title *Why England Slept*. The book became a best seller in both America and England. At 23, John Kennedy had found success as an author. In June 1940, Kennedy graduated from Harvard cum laude (with honors). He stood at a crossroads in his life.

Chapter 2

Drifting

When 23-year-old John F. Kennedy graduated from Harvard in 1940, World War II was raging in Europe. German forces occupied much of Western Europe and were about to occupy Paris. They were sinking British ships and bombing British military bases. In Asia, Japan was at war with China and was threatening other countries.

In the meantime, Jack Kennedy was trying to decide what to do with his life. He had enjoyed writing about England's political scene, so he considered becoming a journalist. He also considered becoming a teacher or a lawyer. In September 1940, he arranged to audit courses (attend class without receiving credit) in the business school at Stanford University in California. A few weeks after Kennedy arrived at Stanford, President Roosevelt signed the Selective Training and Service Act. This law required young men to register for duty in the armed forces. After registration, men were eligible to be *drafted* (called to active duty in the military) if they were needed in time of war.

Still, the United States remained neutral in the war, and the American people were divided on what actions the country should take. The Kennedy family was also divided. Joseph Kennedy Sr. was an *isolationist* (a person who opposes alliances with other countries and involvement in foreign wars). He believed that the United States should remain neutral, and even suggested that Britain should begin talks with Germany on ending the fighting. His position was challenged by Britain's new prime minister, Winston Churchill, and by President Roosevelt, who favored giving aid to Britain's war effort. In November 1940, Roosevelt was elected to a third term as president. Soon afterward, he asked for Joseph Kennedy's resignation as ambassador to Britain. Joe Kennedy Jr. agreed with his father's views, but he said that if the United States entered the war, he would fight.

Jack Kennedy disagreed with his father and his brother. He did not want to see the world at war, but he believed that the United States had an obligation to support Britain and France against the dictatorships in Germany and Italy. Like his brother, he was willing to fight. What worried him was that if he was called for duty, he might be rejected because of his medical problems. He knew he could not be an onlooker while other young men risked their lives in battle, and he worried that if he was rejected, people would think he was shirking his responsibilities. "They will never take me in the Army," he wrote in a letter to a friend. "And yet if I don't go, it will look quite bad."

After about three months at Stanford, Kennedy had lost his interest in business school. He traveled to his family's large vacation home in Palm Beach, Florida. That summer, the Kennedy family was dealing with a family tragedy. Rosemary Kennedy, just a year younger than Jack, had grown up to be a beautiful young woman, but from childhood she had been mentally retarded. In 1941, she was living in a convent school in Washington, D.C., when she became moody and defiant. Joseph Kennedy Sr., afraid that some harm could come to her, arranged for an operation called a lobotomy, in which a small part of the brain is destroyed to make the patient calmer and easier to manage. The operation went terribly wrong. Rosemary was left with the mentality of an infant and was unable to care for herself. The Kennedy family was deeply upset by the incident. Rosemary was placed in a home for the mentally retarded in Wisconsin, where she lived for more than 60 years.

PT Boat Skipper

By June 1941, Joe Kennedy Jr., convinced that the United States would soon be at war, volunteered for duty in the U.S. Navy. Feeling that he could not let his older brother outperform him, Jack Kennedy was almost frantic to get into uniform. He may have taken physical exams for the army and the navy (no records survive). If he did take the physicals, he was not accepted.

Finally, Jack asked his father for help. The elder Kennedy was terrified of what might happen to his sons in combat, but he understood their fierce desire to join in the fight. He used his political influence, and on August 5, 1941, John F. Kennedy was accepted into the navy with the rank of *ensign*, the lowest officer rank. The United States had not yet entered the war, but there was work for a college-trained officer. Kennedy was assigned to an office in Washington, D.C., where he helped gather intelligence about the Japanese buildup for war in the Pacific. While the work was important, Jack found it boring.

Then on December 7, 1941, waves of Japanese bombers appeared over the U.S. naval base at Pearl Harbor, in Hawaii. Caught by surprise early on a Sunday morning, the Americans put up little resistance. Within a few hours, dozens of ships and 300 planes were destroyed or damaged, and nearly 2,400 U.S. troops were killed. The following day, the U.S. Congress declared war on Japan. Three days later, Germany and Italy declared war on the United States and Congress declared war on Germany and Italy.

Even after war was declared, Kennedy remained stuck in his office job in Washington. Finally, in July 1942, he was granted a transfer to sea duty and was sent to midshipmen's school to train for sea duty. During his training, the mid-

The battleships USS *West Virginia* and *Tennessee* burn to the waterline after the Japanese bombed the fleet at Pearl Harbor, Hawaii, on December 7, 1941. The attack brought the United States into World War II.

shipmen received a visit from Captain John Bulkeley, commander of the famous patrol torpedo (PT) boat squadron. In April, Bulkeley and his PT squadron had rescued U.S. General Douglas MacArthur and his family and staff from the Philippine Islands after Japanese forces overran his base there. Now he was

A PT boat speeds through the waters of the South Pacific in 1943. Jack Kennedy would become the skipper of *PT-109.*

looking for volunteers. He hoped to build a large squadron of PT boats, small, swift vessels that could attack slower, larger ships and then escape before the enemy could react.

Kennedy was an experienced sailor of small craft, having spent many summer days on the waters near his family's vacation home on Cape Cod in Massachusetts. He was also intrigued by the possibility that he could command his own vessel. He volunteered for the PT squadron, and in October 1942, began an eight-week course at the PT training school in Melville, Rhode Island.

PT-109

After completing his training, Kennedy was assigned as an instructor at the training school. This was not what he wanted. He wanted to go into combat. Finally, with the help of a Massachusetts political leader, he gained assignment to combat duty early in 1943 and made his way to the South Pacific.

Kennedy was assigned as "skipper" of *PT-109*, in command of a crew of twelve.

Fast Facts

WORLD WAR II

What: War to stop the aggression of the Axis powers, which were seeking world domination

When: 1939–1945

Who: The Axis powers included Germany, Italy, and Japan. The Allied powers included Britain, France, the Soviet Union, the United States, China, Australia, Canada, and many other nations.

Where: In Europe (including the Soviet Union), North Africa, Asia, and on the Atlantic and Pacific Oceans

Why: The Axis powers attacked neighboring countries, seeking world domination, territory for expansion, and natural resources.

Outcome: Allied forces gradually surrounded Axis countries and recovered conquered territories, then attacked the Axis countries themselves. Italy surrendered in 1943. Germany surrendered May 7, 1945, after Allied forces entered Berlin, the German capital. Japan surrendered August 14, 1945, after the U.S. dropped atomic bombs on the Japanese cities of Hiroshima and Nagasaki. Germany was occupied by the main Allied powers, and Japan was governed by U.S. occupation forces.

Early in the morning on August 2, 1943, *PT-109* was moving slowly through the waters near the Solomon Islands north and east of Australia. Kennedy and his crew were on patrol, scouting for Japanese warships. At about 2 a.m., the ship was idling along with only one of its three engines running. Kennedy wanted to keep noise to a minimum so the enemy wouldn't detect his boat. All around, Japanese warships moved through the night, ferrying men and supplies to nearby battles. Suddenly, the Japanese destroyer *Amagiri* loomed out of the darkness. The huge warship was bearing down on *PT-109* at full speed. Kennedy, at the boat's controls, could not avoid a collision. In seconds, *Amagiri*'s knifelike bow sliced the PT boat in half. Two of the crewmen on board were never found. Kennedy and ten others survived, clinging to part of the PT boat that was still barely afloat.

At dawn, Kennedy surveyed their situation, and realized he and his men would have to swim to safety. That afternoon, they headed for the nearest island, more than three miles (5 kilometers) away. The boat's engineer, Patrick Henry McMahon, had been badly burned. To get him to the island, Kennedy towed him, using his teeth to hold a strap of McMahon's life jacket. Kennedy himself was in a great deal of pain. He had been thrown to the deck when *PT-109* was rammed, aggravating his old back injury.

Kennedy, at far right, poses with crew members of *PT-109* before the ship was sunk in a collision with a much larger Japanese battleship.

The survivors crawled ashore on Plum Pudding Island, a tiny dot in the ocean covered with birds and bird droppings. Exhausted and thirsty, they found no food or fresh water on the island. Kennedy concluded that the men must make another long swim to a larger island, on which they could see a few palm trees. The next day the men set out. Once again, Kennedy towed McMahon. On this larger island, called Olasana, the men found coconut palms that could supply them with coconut milk and meat. They were still not safe, however. Survival would be difficult, and several of the men needed medical attention.

The next day, Kennedy and a fellow officer, Barney Ross, set out for yet another island, named Cross Island. There they found a one-man canoe, a small drum of fresh water, and some crackers. They also spotted two native islanders in a canoe that paddled away. Ross, exhausted, fell asleep on the sand. Kennedy used the canoe to carry the crackers and water back to his men on Olasana. There, he discovered that the two islanders, named Biuku and Eroni, were sitting on the beach with the rest of his men. The islanders had also paddled from Cross to Olasana. Now they took Kennedy back to Cross Island to rescue Barney Ross.

Using a sheath knife, Kennedy scratched a message on a coconut and gave it to the islanders. It said, "Native knows posit [position]—he can pilot—11 alive—need small boat—Kennedy." He told them to take the message to Rendova

Island, the main base for the PT boats in the area. The natives quickly paddled off, carrying the message. Within 48 hours, a rescue party arrived, and Kennedy and his crew were safe.

For his role in saving his crew, Jack Kennedy became a hero in the pages of major newspapers across America. He was awarded the Navy and Marine Corps Medal for his bravery. Years later, the story of his courage and resourcefulness following the sinking of his PT boat would help propel John F. Kennedy into the White House.

Returning Home

Following the sinking of *PT-109* in August 1943, Kennedy returned to action in a different PT boat. By early November, however, it was obvious that Kennedy was seriously ill. He suffered from malaria (a tropical disease transmitted by mosquitoes) and from stomach problems, almost certainly caused by an ulcer. In addition, his aggravated back injury caused him almost constant pain.

In December 1943, Kennedy was ordered home. After receiving medical treatment, he was assigned to a training squadron in Miami, Florida. In June 1944, he had surgery to repair the damage in his back. Instead of helping, the operation made the problem worse. His back pain was so intense that he had to take painkilling drugs simply to function.

As he was recovering, Kennedy met John Hersey, a young correspondent whose stories about the war would make him world famous. Hersey wrote a long article about Kennedy and *PT-109*. Called "Survival," it was published in the *New Yorker* magazine. Not long afterward, a shorter version of it appeared in the *Reader's Digest*, a magazine that was read by millions of Americans. In this way, John F. Kennedy became one of the war heroes who gained national fame for his bravery and courage.

While Jack was in the South Pacific, Joe Kennedy Jr. was sent to England as a pilot. To his dismay, he was assigned to fly routine patrols off the coast of France. The duty was dull and offered little chance for heroism. Now Joe felt the sting of competition. When Jack gained widespread attention for his war exploits, Joe wanted to prove that he too was a hero.

In August 1944, he flew a dangerous mission as copilot of a plane packed with explosives. The plan called for the copilots to fly over the English Channel, then bail out and parachute to the water, where they would be rescued by an Allied ship. The pilotless plane, guided by radio signals, would crash into a target in Nazi-held Europe. The plan went disastrously wrong, however. As the heavily loaded plane climbed into the sky, it suddenly exploded. No traces of Kennedy or his copilot were ever found.

Joe Kennedy Jr. in his pilot's gear in England. He died in action in 1944.

The Kennedy family was devastated by Joe's death. In the following months, Jack interviewed people who knew Joe, and wrote a book called *As We Remember Joe*. Even as he worked on the memorial to his brother, however, he was in and out of the hospital. He had several minor operations and treatments for his back and his stomach ailments. Finally, in April 1945, he was discharged from the U.S. Navy.

Chapter 3

Candidate Kennedy

Joseph Kennedy Sr. was deeply affected by his oldest son's death. Ever since his own political career ended with his resignation as ambassador, Kennedy had been planning for the day when Joe Jr. would enter politics and perhaps become America's first Irish Catholic president. Now everything had changed. Suddenly it was Jack's duty to make his father's political dreams come true. Jack Kennedy was willing to take on the task. During much of 1945 and early 1946, he prepared. He wrote magazine and newspaper articles about politics and world affairs to gain attention as a serious thinker. He spoke to groups of voters in Boston and gave interviews to newspapers.

In April 1946, 28-year-old John Kennedy announced that he would seek the Democratic nomination for Congress as a candidate in the Massachusetts 11th congressional district, the same congressional seat that had

once been held by his maternal grandfather, Honey Fitz. To win the nomination, he

had to win the *primary election*, in which Democratic voters in the district picked

Young congressional candidate Jack Kennedy poses with his famous grandfather "Honey Fitz" Fitzgerald (left) and his father, Joseph Kennedy Sr.

their nominee to run in the general election. Nobody worked harder to guarantee Kennedy's success than his father. Joseph Kennedy used his political influence to help create a powerful political organization for his son and spent thousands of dollars on the campaign.

John Kennedy proved to be a good campaigner. Speaking to young voters, he emphasized that he was a veteran asking other veterans to vote for him. Even though he was skinny and looked ill, he found that women voters responded to him. He could be serious, but he had an infectious grin and could poke fun at himself. In addition, he worked hard at campaigning.

Other members of the family also worked hard to get Jack elected. His mother and sisters Eunice, Pat, and Jean hosted tea parties and meetings. They talked to anyone who would listen about Jack's war record and what he would do for voters. His younger brother Bobby, home from the navy, was a tireless campaigner.

On primary day, Kennedy outperformed all nine of the other candidates, winning 22,000 votes, nearly twice as many as his nearest competitor. In the heavily Democratic 11th district, the primary was the hard part. In the general election, he easily defeated the Republican candidate and gained election to the U.S. Congress at the age of 29.

Kennedy and his parents beam while supporters in South Boston celebrate his election to Congress in 1946.

Congressman Kennedy

In January 1947, Kennedy took his seat in the House of Representatives. He looked so young and dressed so casually that he was sometimes mistaken for one of the congressional *pages* (high school students who to carry messages and run errands for representatives in Congress). His youth, his family connections, and his status as a war hero made him newsworthy. Yet Kennedy joined many other notable representatives. One of his fellow freshman congressmen, representing a district in Southern California, was Richard Nixon. Among Democrats, one veteran, serving his fifth term in the House, was Lyndon B. Johnson of Texas.

In September 1947, Kennedy traveled to Ireland to visit his sister Kathleen. After visiting New Ross, the Irish town that had been home to his ancestors, he flew on to London. In London, he fell gravely ill and was rushed to the hospital. During this stay, an English doctor determined that Kennedy was suffering from Addison's disease.

At the time, Addison's was a mysterious disease that was often fatal. It occurs when the two adrenal glands (one perched on each kidney) fail to produce important hormones which affect important bodily processes, including digestion, resisting disease, and rebuilding damaged tissues after injury. Fortunately, medical researchers had recently learned how to produce those hormones cheaply

Kennedy's Health

John Kennedy had been sickly since childhood. He seemed always to be recovering from some illness or injury. Many of his early illnesses were difficult to explain and treat, and he seemed to recover slowly. Many of these earlier ailments may have been caused by or complicated by Addison's disease, which he may have had since he was a boy.

★★☆

outside the body. For the rest of his life, Kennedy relied on regular doses of powerful hormonal drugs to remain healthy.

Eager to protect his political future and wanting to be perceived as a healthy young man, Kennedy kept his medical problems secret. Only his family and a few close advisers knew how sick he was or had any idea of his use of medications. At the same time, Jack seemed to refuse facing up to his own sicknesses. "He went along for many years thinking to himself—or at least trying to make others think—that he was a strong, robust, quite healthy person," his mother, Rose, said.

In 1948 tragedy struck the Kennedy family yet again. Just a year after Jack Kennedy visited his sister Kathleen in Ireland, she was killed in a plane crash in France. Jack Kennedy was devastated by the death of his sister, and he grieved all over again for the death of his brother Joe. "The thing about Kathleen and Joe was their tremendous vitality," he said. He just could not understand how his brother and sister, so filled with life, could possibly be taken from the world so suddenly and so senselessly. "How can there possibly be any purpose in her death?" he asked again and again.

John Kennedy seemed to be changed by the deaths of his brother and sister. He began to live life more intensely. A friend, Chuck Spalding, said that Kennedy seemed aware that death was waiting for him. So, Spalding said, Kennedy "tried to burn bright, he tried to wring as much out of things as he could."

Meanwhile, as a member of Congress, Kennedy worked for his constituents. Though he typically supported the Democratic administration of President Harry Truman, he was not afraid to show his independence. At one point, he refused to support an application to pardon a popular Massachusetts Democrat

Congressman Kennedy with President Harry Truman. Kennedy would become president eight years after Truman left office.

Harry S. Truman

Harry S. Truman (1884–1972) had served as a senator from Missouri in the 1930s and 1940s. In 1944 he was elected vice president on the ticket with President Franklin D. Roosevelt. Less than three months after Truman took office, Roosevelt died and Truman became president. In 1948 he was elected to a full term. Truman was not always popular as president, but he proved himself an able leader in difficult times. When he made a bad decision, he refused to blame it on others, insisting that the president had final responsibility for his administration. He kept a sign on his desk that emphasized the point. It said, "The buck stops here." Kennedy would have reason to recall Truman's attitude when some of his own White House actions proved to be unwise.

☆ ☆ ☆

because he believed the man did not deserve a pardon. He also joined with Republicans who believed that President Harry Truman was not doing enough to fight the Communists in China.

Kennedy was easily re-elected to the House in 1948 and again in 1950, but he was not happy as a congressman. Bills moved slowly through the legislative process, and endless hours were taken up with tiresome debates and arguments. He felt too much time was wasted and not enough was accomplished. During his third term, he began considering higher office.

In April 1952, Kennedy announced he would seek the U.S. Senate seat held by Republican Senator Henry Cabot Lodge II. The Lodge family was one of the most famous and respected in Massachusetts. In fact, Lodge's grandfather had defeated Kennedy's grandfather, Honey Fitz, in a campaign for the Senate almost 40 years earlier. The younger Lodge, a popular and experienced politician, seemed certain to win re-election in 1952.

Once again, Joseph Kennedy's money played a major role in the campaign. With his huge family bankroll, Jack Kennedy was able to buy time for dozens of radio and television ads. This was the first election season in which candidates could reach a majority of voters through television. In addition, Kennedy money may have helped gain an endorsement from a Boston newspaper. The Boston *Post* was in financial trouble. Soon after Joseph Kennedy made a $500,000 loan to the paper, it urged its readers to support Jack Kennedy for the Senate.

Once again, the whole Kennedy clan campaigned. Kennedy's mother and sisters were particularly helpful in attracting the votes of women. They hosted a series of teas in some of the finest hotels in the state. There the guests had a chance to meet the candidate and chat with the Kennedy family. Many left convinced that Jack Kennedy belonged in the Senate. Kennedy himself was a tireless campaigner. Despite his back problems he worked from early in the morning until

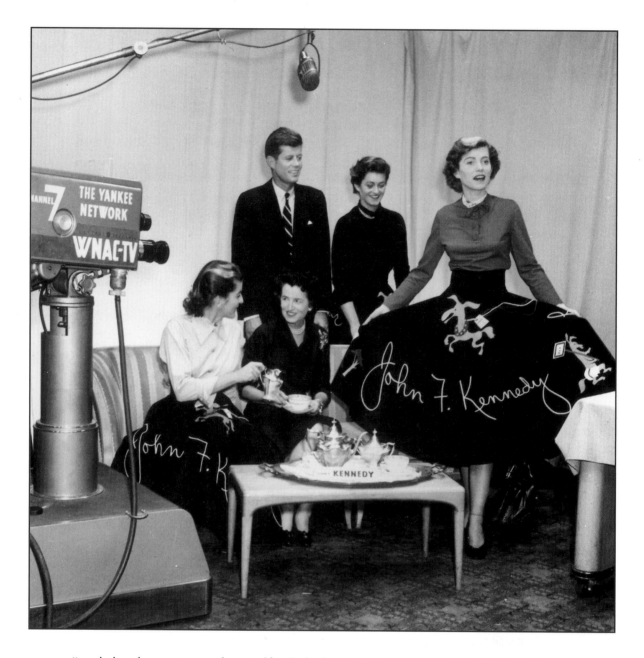

Kennedy shows the campaign support he received from his family during his run for the U.S. Senate in 1952. His mother is seated at center in front of the special Kennedy tea service, while three of his sisters display full skirts featuring the Kennedy signature.

late at night. He traveled to speak, to shake hands, and to meet political leaders around the state.

Election day, November 4, 1952, was a nail-biter. The Democratic candidate for president, Adlai Stevenson, went down to defeat, losing to the popular Republican, Dwight D. Eisenhower. In Massachusetts, Kennedy and Lodge ran neck and neck until late in the day. Then, slowly, the tide turned in Kennedy's favor. Still, the election was not decided until early the next morning. Kennedy had upset Lodge. Now 35-year-old John F. Kennedy represented the whole state of Massachusetts in the United States Senate, one step nearer to the center of power.

John F. Kennedy was sworn in as the new senator from Massachusetts on January 20, 1953. Of the 96 Senate seats, Democrats held 47, and Republicans held 49. As a freshman senator and a member of the minority party, Kennedy was

Kennedy's Team

As a senator, Kennedy set about building an organization to help him accomplish as much as he could in Washington. One of the people he hired was Theodore Sorensen, a 24-year-old lawyer from Nebraska. Another was Evelyn Lincoln, his personal secretary. Both Sorensen and Mrs. Lincoln, as Kennedy always referred to her, provided valuable help and support to him as a senator and later as president.

☆★☆

starting at the bottom. Still, Kennedy had promised to do more for the people of Massachusetts than Henry Cabot Lodge had done. He set out to make good on that promise, introducing proposals that would help such Massachusetts industries as fishing and textile manufacturing. Eventually, almost all the proposals Kennedy made were enacted into law.

Jacqueline Bouvier Kennedy ————————

By the time John Kennedy was elected to the Senate, he had begun to date Jacqueline Bouvier. Nearly everyone called her Jackie, even though she hated the nickname. Twelve years younger than Jack, she was a striking young woman with dark, luxuriant hair and deep brown eyes. She came from a wealthy and cultivated family. She had studied at Vassar College and the Sorbonne in Paris, France, and graduated in 1951 from George Washington University in Washington, D.C. Cultured and artistic, she spoke fluent French, Italian, and Spanish.

In May 1953, when Jackie was in London, Jack sent a telegram asking her to marry him. She soon agreed, and they were married on September 12, 1953, at St. Mary's Catholic Church, in fashionable Newport, Rhode Island. Senator Kennedy and his beautiful young wife were soon recognized as one of the most charming and intelligent couples in Washington. In 1957, Jackie gave birth to a baby girl, whom the couple named Caroline Bouvier Kennedy.

Jack Kennedy and his fiancée Jacqueline Bouvier in May 1953. Four months later, they were married in fashionable Newport, Rhode Island.

National Defense

In June 1953, United Nations forces in Korea signed an armistice ending the Korean conflict. Three years earlier, the Communist government of North Korea had invaded South Korea, whose government was supported by the United States. U.N. forces (mainly from the United States) had landed in South Korea to drive out the North Korean invaders. After bitter fighting, they had driven the Communist forces back into North Korea. Americans were relieved that the war was over, but they remained deeply concerned about the dangers of Communist aggression around the world.

Senator Jack Kennedy shared these concerns. He believed strongly that America had to be prepared for war to maintain peace. He was ready to speak out about what he believed. At the same time, he knew that making speeches about foreign affairs was a good way to gain national attention. As one of his journalist friends put it, such speeches would put his "eager boyish puss" in newspapers and magazines.

Communism at Home

Americans were also concerned that Communists might be a danger at home. Senator Joseph McCarthy of Wisconsin was a leading critic of the federal government, claiming that it was "soft on Communism." He claimed that there were hundreds of secret Communists in sensitive government positions. In 1953 McCarthy became chairman of the Senate's Committee on Government Operations, which he used as a forum for investigating Communist influence in the government.

McCarthy was a longtime friend of the Kennedy family, and Senator Jack Kennedy was assigned a seat on McCarthy's committee. His younger brother, Bobby Kennedy, became minority *counsel* (legal adviser) to the committee's investigations subcommittee. At first the Kennedy brothers supported McCarthy's efforts to find Communists in the government, but they soon realized that McCarthy was misusing his powers and making unfounded accusations against innocent people. In 1954, Democrats on the committee began to withdraw from its investigations.

More Suffering

Jack Kennedy was suffering once again from severe back pain. Years later, his brother Robert recalled, "At least one half of the days he spent on this earth were days of intense physical pain."

By mid-1954, he was suffering as never before. He got around on crutches because walking was too painful. His staff often carried him up and down stairs in buildings that had no elevators. Doctors told him that without surgery he might soon be unable to walk. Doctors warned Kennedy that the surgery would be risky because of his Addison's disease, but even they did not realize how risky it would be.

"Jack was determined to have the operation," Rose Kennedy said later. "He told his father that . . . he would rather be dead than spend the rest of his life hobbling on crutches and paralyzed by pain." On October 10, 1954, Kennedy entered a hospital in New York and on October 21 doctors performed the surgery.

Following the operation, an infection set in, and Kennedy was near death. A priest was called to administer the last rites of the church, but the young senator rallied and began to improve. He remained in the hospital for eight weeks, then was transported to the Kennedy home in Palm Beach, Florida, where he continued his slow recovery. He still lay flat on his back in a special hospital bed and required skilled nursing care. Later he returned to New York for a second operation. He was not well enough to return to Washington until May 1955.

While Kennedy was recovering from his surgery, the U.S. Senate voted to *censure* (officially condemn) Senator McCarthy for his high-handed actions and false accusations of high government officials. The censure effectively ended McCarthy's anti-Communist crusade.

Jack Kennedy arrives at a hospital in New York in October 1954 for surgery to repair his back injury. He nearly died after the operation and did not return to the Senate until May 1955.

Profiles in Courage

As Kennedy recuperated from surgery, he decided to write a book about senators who took courageous stands during their careers. He ordered stacks of books and documents from the Library of Congress and began his reading while still lying flat on his back. He worked closely with his staff in Washington, especially with Ted Sorensen, who was an experienced writer and editor. Kennedy dictated chapter drafts, and Sorensen revised and improved them. Later, when he was able to sit up, Kennedy revised and rewrote Sorensen's drafts. The finished book was published in 1957 by a leading New York publisher under the title *Profiles in Courage*. Later that year, it was awarded the Pulitzer Prize for biography and gained a wide audience.

Chapter 4

Vice Presidential Hopeful ——————

When Kennedy returned to the Senate after his hospitalization, he was determined to make a name as an important politician. He tried to get a seat on the Foreign Relations Committee, where he could help to shape America's foreign policy. Instead, he was assigned to the Labor and Public Welfare Committee. There he began to speak out in favor of increasing the minimum wage from 75¢ to $1.00 an hour (from about $3.90 to $5.20 an hour in current value) as a way to help the working poor. Kennedy and other supporters managed to gain passage of the increase in early 1956.

Kennedy was also keeping his eye on Democratic politics. Although he was not up for re-election, 1956 was a presidential election year. When the well-known Hollywood writer Dore Shary asked Kennedy to speak the narration for a Democratic campaign film, Kennedy quickly agreed. This film, called "The Pursuit of Happiness,"

At the 1956 Democratic convention, Kennedy supporters wave signs urging his nomination for vice president to run with presidential candidate Adlai Stevenson. Kennedy lost the nomination to Tennessee senator Estes Kefauver.

was shown at the 1956 Democratic convention in Chicago and made Kennedy an instant star.

The next day, Adlai E. Stevenson of Illinois was nominated for the second time to run for president against Republican Dwight Eisenhower. Stevenson left the choice of a vice presidential candidate to the convention delegates. Kennedy and his aides worked hard to win the nomination, but when the delegates began voting, he came up short. When it became clear that the majority favored Senator Estes Kefauver of Tennessee, Kennedy made his way to the rostrum at the front of the convention hall. Flashing his infectious grin, Kennedy asked delegates to make Kefauver's nomination unanimous. Kennedy's ability to smile in defeat endeared him to millions of people who watched on television.

Kennedy was disappointed about his defeat by Kefauver. Joseph Kennedy, however, was not unhappy with the results. He felt sure that Stevenson and Kefauver would be defeated by President Eisenhower and Vice President Nixon in the general election. "Jack's better off without [the nomination]," he said. "He's better off running for the top spot in '60."

In November, as Joseph Kennedy predicted, Republicans Eisenhower and Nixon easily won re-election. John Kennedy came to agree with his father. Even without the vice-presidential nomination, his exposure at the 1956 convention set up a successful run for the presidency just four years later.

The Civil Rights Movement ———————

After John F. Kennedy's unsuccessful try for the vice presidential nomination in 1956, he set his sights on the presidency. His father and mother and his brothers and sisters were all solidly behind his decision. It was, after all, what they had all been preparing for ever since Joe Kennedy Jr. had died in World War II.

Kennedy was a rising star in the Democratic party. Invitations to speak to groups across the nation came streaming into his office. In 1957 and 1958, he spoke to more than 350 groups large and small across the country. One of his topics was *civil rights* for African Americans (legal rights to be treated equally with other citizens). African Americans in the South were *segregated* (kept separate by law) in the South. They were not allowed to stay in hotels or eat in restaurants patronized by white people, and they were required to sit in separate sections in buses and movie theaters. They attended separate all-black schools. Kennedy believed that legal segregation was not just wrong but evil. Yet he knew that taking a public stand was risky. At the time, the Democratic party was strongest among white voters in the southern states, and he would need their support to gain the presidency.

In 1954, the U.S. Supreme Court had ruled that separate public schools for whites and African Americans were unconstitutional. Then, late in 1955, Rosa Parks, a black woman in Montgomery, Alabama, was arrested for refusing to sit in the blacks-only section of a city bus. Martin Luther King Jr., a young black pastor in Montgomery, helped organize a black *boycott*, refusing to use the Montgomery buses or shop at white-owned businesses until segregation of buses was ended. After more than a year, Montgomery bus companies agreed.

In the fall of 1957, the first African American students arrived to enroll at Central High School in Little Rock, Arkansas. They were met by an angry crowd of white people, who threatened the black students and prevented them from reg-

istering. When the Arkansas governor refused to enforce the court-ordered integration of the school, President Eisenhower sent U.S. troops to escort black students into the building. Soon afterward, Eisenhower's attorney general, Herbert Brownell, introduced a new civil rights act for passage by Congress.

Senator Kennedy supported the new legislation, which provided for a new Division of Civil Rights in the Department of Justice and a federal Civil Rights Commission. Southern Democrats fiercely opposed the act and succeeded in watering

Senator Kennedy meets with Senate majority leader Lyndon B. Johnson in 1957 during the debate on the Civil Rights Act that passed later that year.

down many of its provisions, but the Civil Rights Act passed. It was the first civil rights legislation passed by Congress since 1875.

Senate Rackets Committee ———————

At the same time, Kennedy was named a member of a special committee to investigate corruption and the influence of organized crime in labor unions. Known as the Senate Rackets Committee, it held public hearings that were televised across the nation. They produced some of the most dramatic "theater" ever seen as leaders of corrupt unions snarled at the members of the committee and at the cameras.

As a consequence of these hearings, Kennedy became even more of a television star. So did his brother, Bobby Kennedy, who was the committee's chief lawyer. Another consequence was that the accused union leaders became enemies of all the Kennedys.

Re-election to the Senate ———————

In 1958, Kennedy ran for election to another six-year term in the U.S. Senate. Massachusetts Republicans, knowing that they could not defeat Kennedy, ran a virtually unknown candidate. Kennedy won with 874,000 votes to his opponent's 314,000.

Jack and Jackie Kennedy meet with supporters in 1958 after he won a second term in the U.S. Senate.

The victory gave Kennedy a secure place from which to campaign for the presidency two years later.

Once again, he accepted invitations to speak all over the country. He spent almost every weekend on the road. He spoke to voters about issues of national importance as he worked to prove he was a serious candidate. His grueling schedule helped convince Kennedy that he could stand the rigors of a national

Family Life

To the public, Jack and Jacqueline Kennedy seemed to be a perfect couple, like something out of a fairy tale. With the birth of their daughter Caroline in 1957, they became a magical young family. This public impression continued through Kennedy's presidency. It was later revealed, however, that the truth was somewhat different. Kennedy often left his wife home alone while he traveled to speaking engagements and to spend time off with old friends. There was evidence that Kennedy had affairs with many other women during his travels. His behavior hurt his wife terribly.

It was no secret to her close friends that Jackie was unhappy in her marriage. Still, she presented a happy picture to the outside world and continued to support Jack's ambitions for higher office. Jack and Jackie knew that their glamorous image was important to their success and continued to conceal unhappy aspects of their lives.

☆ ☆ ☆

campaign. "I know I'll never be more than eighty to eighty-five percent healthy," he told a friend. "But as long as I know that, I'm all right."

Kennedy also prepared to make use of his youth and good looks. He realized that television was a powerful force in campaigning. To be ready, he consulted with a portrait photographer to determine what poses and angles made him look best, how to hold his head to look strong and serious, and how to appear like a statesman.

Running for President

On January 2, 1960, 42-year-old John Fitzgerald Kennedy announced that he was seeking the office of president. Kennedy was not the only Democrat seeking the nomination. Among his competitors were Senator Hubert H. Humphrey Jr., a widely admired senator from Minnesota, and Senator Lyndon B. Johnson of Texas, the powerful Senate majority leader. Adlai E. Stevenson, who had run twice against Eisenhower, was also in the running. It soon became clear, however, that the main contest would be between Kennedy and Humphrey.

The first goal was to win state primary elections, which would give Kennedy delegates firmly pledged to vote for his nomination at the national convention. Once again, the Kennedy organization swung into action. The first real battle occurred in Wisconsin. The Kennedy "machine" and its money helped give Kennedy a lopsided victory over Humphrey.

The most crucial battleground was West Virginia. In Wisconsin, Kennedy could rely on a large Roman Catholic population to vote for him. In West Virginia, fewer than 5 percent of the voters were Catholic, and the election would be a test of the "religious issue." Although Humphrey never mentioned the issue, his supporters suggested that a Roman Catholic could never be elected as president. The Kennedy organization answered by pouring time and money into their campaign. Kennedy spent days campaigning there, appearing often on local television. Members of his family came to visit with West Virginia voters. Meanwhile, Kennedy volunteers throughout the state visited individual homes, asking for support. Humphrey devoted less attention to the state, leaving much of the campaigning to local supporters. On election night, May 10, 1960, Kennedy's charm and his campaign muscle won a convincing victory and brightened the chance that he would win the nomination in July.

The Democratic Convention

The Democratic party met in Los Angeles, California, in early July to nominate candidates for president and vice president. By now, Kennedy had a group of

Arriving in Los Angeles for the 1960 Democratic convention, Jack Kennedy is mobbed by fans and supporters.

experienced political workers on his team, including his brother Bobby, who visited state delegations, using pleas, deals, and threats to gain support. Joseph Kennedy Sr. was also at work. He convinced Mayor Richard Daley of Chicago to help shift the votes of Illinois delegates from Stevenson to Kennedy. Soon, other state delegations followed suit. Kennedy won the nomination on the first ballot, gaining 806 votes. Lyndon Johnson, who had not campaigned actively because of his work as Senate majority leader, came in second, with 409.

Then Kennedy stepped before delegates and TV cameras to accept the nomination. His speech that night thrilled the convention and some 35 million people who watched on television. He said, "We stand today at the edge of a New Frontier—the frontier of the 1960s—a frontier of unknown opportunities and perils—a frontier of unfulfilled hopes and threats." The idea of a "New Frontier" would become a central theme of his campaign.

The next step was choosing a vice presidential candidate. Kennedy wanted Lyndon Johnson. Not all his advisers agreed. Bobby Kennedy could hardly stand to be in the same room with Johnson. Jack Kennedy worried only that Johnson might refuse his offer. As majority leader of the Senate, Johnson was one of the most powerful men in the country. He would have to give up his power in the Senate for a job that had little power.

Kennedy asked Lyndon Johnson to be his vice-presidential nominee. After the election, he visited the Johnson ranch in Texas.

"I want Lyndon," Kennedy said at one point on the day he was nominated. "But I'd never want to offer it and have him turn me down. . . . Lyndon's the natural choice, and with him on the ticket, there's no way we could lose." The next day, Kennedy offered Johnson the vice presidential nomination and Johnson accepted.

The next month, as expected, the Republicans named the current vice president, Richard Nixon, as their presidential candidate. Nixon's running mate was Henry Cabot Lodge of Massachusetts, the same man Kennedy had beaten in his run for the Senate in 1952.

Chapter 5

Campaign for the Presidency

During the 1960 campaign, Kennedy and Nixon presented very similar plans for the country. Both men talked of progress and change, with Kennedy hitting the idea of a New Frontier again and again. Ultimately, the campaign became a debate about experience. Though both men had come to Congress in the same year, Nixon tried to focus voters' attention on his eight years of experience as Eisenhower's vice president. For a time, Nixon's strategy seemed to be working. Kennedy looked young, almost boyish. That made him vulnerable to Nixon's attacks and swung support behind the Republican candidate.

For Kennedy, one of the most difficult issues was his religious affiliation. He had already proved in West Virginia that he could win the support of Protestant voters, but some influential Protestant leaders believed that a Roman Catholic should never be elected president.

The Houston Ministerial Association had raised doubts about electing a Roman Catholic as president. Kennedy appeared in person to address their concerns.

They suggested that a Catholic is bound to follow the dictates of the Roman Catholic leadership and might be required, because of his faith, to accept orders from the Pope, the head of the Church. Instead of ducking the issue, Kennedy decided to confront it head on, and to do so on television.

During a televised appearance in Houston before the Houston Ministerial Association, a group of Protestant church leaders, Kennedy said that he supported the separation of church and state. He added that he was against federal funding of private religious schools. "I am not the Catholic candidate for president," he said. "I am the Democratic party's candidate for president, who happens also to be a Catholic. I do not speak for my church on public matters . . . and my church does not speak for me." For many who saw his speech or read it later, his clear statement put the issue to rest.

The Debates

Knowing he had to counter voter impressions that he was too young and inexperienced for the presidency, Kennedy issued a challenge to Nixon. He offered to debate the Republican candidate, face-to-face, on national television. Never before had presidential candidates debated where they could be seen by millions of voters. The two campaign teams finally agreed on four debates between late September and late October.

On September 26, 1960, some 70 million Americans tuned in to watch the first debate, nearly two-thirds of the country's adult population. As the debate progressed, Kennedy looked and sounded like a leader. Nixon looked unshaven, sweaty, and uncomfortable. Historian Theodore H. White, who watched the

Candidates John Kennedy and Richard Nixon after the very first televised presidential debate in September 1960.

debate, said that Kennedy appeared "calm and nerveless." The vice president seemed "tense, almost frightened, at turns glowering, and occasionally haggard-looking to the point of sickness."

In fact, Nixon had been ill. Only five days earlier he had left the hospital after treatment for an infection in one of his legs. After leaving the hospital, he came down with the flu. The night of the debate, he had also refused to allow use of makeup on his face. The contrast in the appearance of the two candidates that night was a turning point in the campaign. Nixon looked healthier in the remaining three debates, but he was never able to regain his early momentum.

During the campaign, civil rights leader Martin Luther King Jr. was jailed in Albany, Georgia. His supporters sent pleas to both candidates for help to gain his release. Kennedy sent his brother Bobby to negotiate King's release on bail, and his actions gained the support of many African Americans. Before 1960, a majority of African American voters voted for Republicans (and against the southern Democratic leaders who still favored segregation). From 1960 on, increasing majorities of African Americans voted for Democrats.

The Kennedy campaign also gained a boost from the halfhearted way President Eisenhower seemed to support Nixon, his own vice president, in the election. During a press conference, a reporter asked Eisenhower if he could name a major idea of Nixon's that had been adopted during his years as vice president. Eisenhower, taken by surprise, said, "If you gave me a week, maybe I could think of one. I don't remember." The Kennedy campaign used a video recording of that exchange in its television advertising.

Shortly after winning election as president, Kennedy addresses a press conference. Jackie, only weeks from giving birth to their son John Jr., stands at his side.

The election was expected to be close, and it was. When Kennedy grew tired of watching the returns at about 4 o'clock in the morning, the outcome was still not clear. At 9:30 a.m., Ted Sorensen entered Kennedy's bedroom. Jack was sitting up in bed, dressed in pajamas. When Sorensen addressed him as "Mr. President," Kennedy knew for the first time that he had won.

Kennedy won 49.7 percent of the popular vote to Nixon's 49.5 percent. The electoral vote, though, was more clear, with Kennedy winning 303 electoral votes to Nixon's 219. Many in the nation greeted Kennedy's election with anticipation of a new era in which a young, vibrant man would lead the nation.

Inauguration

John F. Kennedy was sworn in as the 35th president of the United States on Friday, January 20, 1961. It was a bitterly cold day in Washington, D.C.

Kennedy, who had spent most of his life preparing for this moment, stood before Earl Warren, the chief justice of the U.S. Supreme Court. He placed his left hand on the Fitzgerald family Bible and raised his right hand to take the oath. In moments he was sworn in as the head of the most powerful nation on Earth. He was, at age 43, the youngest man ever elected to the office. (Theodore Roosevelt, a vice president who became president on the death of William McKinley, was nearly a year younger than Kennedy when he took office in 1901.)

When Kennedy moved to the rostrum to deliver his inaugural speech, he knew his words would help set the tone of his entire first term in office. "Let the word go forth from this time and place," he said, "to friend and foe alike, that the torch has been passed to a new generation of Americans—born in this century, tempered by war, disciplined by a hard and bitter peace."

He spoke of international politics. He spoke of the greatness of America and of his hope that the energy, faith, and devotion of his generation would burn with an energy that could light the world.

"And so, my fellow Americans," he said, "ask not what your country can do for you—ask what you can do for your country. My fellow citizens of the world, ask not what America will do for you, but what together we can do for the freedom of man."

Kennedy delivers his widely acclaimed inaugural address in January 1961. Sitting at the left are Jackie Kennedy, outgoing president Dwight Eisenhower, and Chief Justice Earl Warren. At right are the incoming and outgoing vice presidents, Lyndon Johnson and Richard Nixon. Both Johnson and Nixon would later become president.

Kennedy's speech is considered by many today to be one of the greatest inaugural addresses ever delivered. Almost as soon as it ended, though, the new president found himself facing difficulties at home and overseas.

Kennedy's Cabinet

Kennedy was eager to reassure Republicans who were afraid that a Democrat might take unfriendly actions against business. When he chose his *cabinet*, the heads of major government departments who serve as the president's senior advisers, he chose several Republicans. He named C. Douglas Dillon as secretary of the treasury and Robert S. McNamara, the former president of the Ford Motor Company, as secretary of defense. He also appointed Dean Rusk, president of the large foundation founded by the Republican Rockefeller family, as secretary of state.

One of Kennedy's most controversial appointments was the man he named to serve as attorney general, the nation's highest law enforcement officer and head of the Department of Justice. For this powerful post, Kennedy chose his brother Bobby. He knew people would question his choice. Not only was Bobby the president's brother, he was also only 35 years old, very young to hold a major cabinet post.

Kennedy's choice of his brother Robert to serve as attorney general caused much debate. Robert Kennedy was the first brother of a president ever to serve in the cabinet—and he was only 35 years old.

The First 100 Days

Before the election, Kennedy planned to present to Congress a sweeping legislative program similar to that put forth by Franklin D. Roosevelt in his famous "first 100 days" in 1933. After the election, he decided to act more cautiously.

Still, the White House seemed to buzz with activity in the days following the inauguration.

Kennedy and his staff sent a record number of proposals to the Congress. These included plans to spur economic growth, improve urban housing, reform tax laws, conserve natural resources, provide more aid to education, and provide better medical care for the aged. Congress was slow to act, however, and none of these broad proposals passed. Congress did agree on short-term legislation to help pull the country out of a mild *recession* (economic slowdown).

One action during Kennedy's first weeks caught the nation's imagination. In March 1961, the president established the Peace Corps by executive order and appointed Sargent Shriver (the husband of his sister Eunice) as its first director. The Peace Corps offered young Americans the opportunity to answer Kennedy's call for public service, volunteering to work for two years without pay in needy communities around the world. Peace Corps workers would use their education and skills to encourage literacy, and improve public health and education. Applications poured in. In the first two years, 7,200 volunteers served in 44 countries. The program remains active and popular today, attracting not only young volunteers but retirees. President Jimmy Carter's mother served in the Peace Corp when she was in her late 60s.

President Kennedy greets new members of the Peace Corps, who are about to travel to their overseas assignments.

The Bay of Pigs

Meanwhile, Kennedy was headed for trouble in his dealings with foreign nations. Indeed, the story of Kennedy's presidency is largely a story of one foreign policy crisis after another. In mid-April 1961, an armed force of about 1,500 Cuban *refugees* (people who flee from their country because they fear personal danger or political persecution) landed in Cuba at the Bay of Pigs, hoping to stir up a revolt against the government of Fidel Castro. The United States was not officially involved in the landing, but the Cuban fighters had been trained and equipped with weapons by the U.S. Central Intelligence Agency, the organization responsible for U.S. spying and political action overseas. Clearly the operation was approved by the U.S. government.

The landing proved to be a disaster. Cubans in the surrounding villages did not flock to the "freedom fighters" to help overthrow the Castro government. Instead, they cooperated with the Cuban army to kill the invaders and send the survivors to Cuban prisons. The clumsy action was condemned by friends and foes of the United States. The Soviet Union, which had recently concluded trade agreements with Cuba, considered the invasion a hostile act against one of its allies. In the United States, however, both Democrats and Republicans rallied behind the president.

Fidel Castro

Fidel Castro (1926–) became a political activist and revolutionary in Cuba during the 1950s, opposing the corrupt government of Fulgencio Batista. He was imprisoned from 1951 to 1955, then fled to Mexico, where he organized a revolutionary organization. The next year, he and a small band of followers returned to the mountains of Cuba and began a guerrilla campaign against the government. In 1959, he forced Batista from power and took control of the government. In his early days in power, Castro was applauded by many Americans, who deplored the Batista government. By 1960, however, he was seizing U.S.-owned businesses. When the U.S. government ended the purchase of Cuba's sugar (its main crop), Castro sought a trade agreement and an alliance

Castro reports to Cuban citizens about the Bay of Pigs invasion in 1961. He continued to be an outspoken critic of the United States through his long reign as Cuba's unquestioned leader.

with the Soviet Union. In late 1961 (after the Bay of Pigs invasion), he announced the formation of a Communist state and increased his ties to other Communist nations. In spite of the hostility of the United States, Castro remained in power for more than 45 years.

☆ ☆ ☆

This would not be the last time Cuba posed trouble for Kennedy and the United States. Eighteen months later, another Cuban crisis would almost result in war between America and the Soviet Union.

The Cuban Missile Crisis ——————————

On October 16, 1962, Kennedy was in his bedroom in the White House, enjoying breakfast, when McGeorge Bundy, the president's adviser on national security, knocked on his door and entered. Bundy was carrying a sheaf of photographs. He quickly spread them on the president's bed. The photographs showed Soviet missile bases under construction in Cuba. Once these bases were completed and armed with missiles from Russia, almost all of the mainland United States would be vulnerable to a nuclear attack.

The next few days were frantic ones for Kennedy and his administration. The nation's military leaders and Secretary of Defense Robert McNamara wanted to attack Cuba. Robert Kennedy, the attorney general and Jack's most trusted adviser, was not sure what course of action to take. Ultimately, President Kennedy decided to do everything he could to avoid action that could start a devastating nuclear war.

On the evening of October 22, Kennedy spoke to the American people. Warned that the president's address was of grave importance, nearly 100 million viewers tuned in. In his speech, Kennedy was forceful, but not *belligerent* (war-like). He displayed aerial photographs that revealed the nearly completed missile sites. Then he informed the leader of the Soviet Union, Nikita Khrushchev, and the world that he was willing to risk a war in order to safeguard the United States. "This secret, swift and extraordinary buildup of Communist missiles . . . is a deliberately provocative and unjustified change . . . which cannot be accepted by this country," he said.

Kennedy announced that the United States would *quarantine* (block the delivery of) any offensive military weapons being shipped to Cuba. He called for other steps as well. These included an emergency meeting of the United Nations to discuss the crisis. Finally, Kennedy made an appeal to Khrushchev. He asked the Soviet leader to "halt and eliminate this *clandestine* [secret], reckless and provocative threat to world peace and to stable relations between our two nations."

Over the next few days, the United States positioned its ships to block Soviet ships carrying nuclear missiles to Cuba. The world held its breath as the Soviet ships approached. When they arrived, on October 24, they stopped, turned around, and sailed away.

For the moment, at least, war had been averted. In the White House, Secretary of State Dean Rusk said, "We are eyeball to eyeball, and I think the

In the most dangerous moment of his presidency, Kennedy addresses the nation in October 1962. He reveals that Soviet nuclear missiles have been spotted in Cuba. After a tense standoff, the Soviets agreed to remove the missiles.

other fellow just blinked." Still, the crisis was not over. The Soviets still refused to honor the blockade. America continued to insist that they must honor the blockade and remove their missiles and missile launchers from Cuba.

Neither Kennedy nor Khrushchev wanted to appear weak. Finally, a deal was worked out behind the scenes. In exchange for the Soviets removing their missiles from Cuba, Kennedy agreed to remove U.S. nuclear missiles positioned in Turkey, within striking distance of Moscow. On November 20, the Soviet government announced it would dismantle and withdraw its offensive weapons in Cuba. After that announcement, the United States ended its quarantine, and the crisis came to an end.

Chapter 6

Foreign Policy Victories

After the Cuban missile crisis, President Kennedy was able to score another foreign policy victory. Early in his presidency, he had urged the Soviet Union to agree to a treaty to end nuclear testing in the atmosphere. Scientific tests had shown that radioactive material from earlier tests had drifted around the world and endangered the health of plants, animals, and people everywhere. Khrushchev had turned down the proposal. Now the Soviet premier showed a willingness to negotiate. It took months, but finally, on October 7, 1963, a test ban treaty was signed by the United States, the Soviet Union, and Great Britain. It was later signed by most nations in the world.

Domestic Affairs

Most of Kennedy's time in office was spent dealing with foreign policy issues. He attempted to shape domestic policy, but accomplished little. Congress took no action on his call to spend more money on education. It killed proposals for increased medical aid for the elderly. Congress also killed Kennedy's idea to establish a department of urban affairs.

Once again, civil rights for African Americans demanded attention during Kennedy's term. In June 1963, a federal court ordered the admission of two black students to the University of Alabama in Tuscaloosa. George Wallace, the governor of Alabama, appeared personally to block the enrollment of the students. President Kennedy sent Alabama National Guard troops to the campus to escort and protect the students during registration. That night Kennedy addressed the nation on television. He announced the actions he had taken in Alabama and said,

> One hundred years of delay have passed since President Lincoln freed the slaves, yet their heirs, their grandsons, are not fully free. They are not yet freed from the bonds of injustice. They are not yet freed from social and economic oppression. And this nation, for all its hopes and all its boasts, will not be fully free until all its citizens are free.

Near the end of his speech, he announced that he would submit a broad new civil rights act to the Congress in the following weeks.

The president's speech and the legislation he proposed struck a chord with thousands of supporters of civil rights, black and white alike. They began planning a March on Washington that summer to put pressure on Congress to pass the new legislation. On August 28, at least 200,000 people arrived in the capital city and gathered peacefully on the Mall in Washington facing the Lincoln Memorial. Leading musicians of the day performed and led the huge crowd in song. Major civil rights leaders addressed the crowd. The final speaker was the Reverend Martin Luther King Jr. In his speech, he outlined his personal dream and the dream of the movement he led. He said,

> I have a dream that one day this nation will rise up and live out the true meaning of its creed: "We hold these truths to be self-evident: that all men are created equal." I have a dream that one day on the red hills of Georgia the sons of former slaves and the sons of former slave-owners will be able to sit down together at a table of brotherhood. . . . I have a dream that my four children will one day live in a nation where they will not be judged by the color of their skin but by the content of their character. I have a dream today.

After the demonstration, President Kennedy met with the civil rights leaders. He applauded their goals, but could not promise that the new civil rights act would be passed promptly. It would face a long, difficult debate in Congress. In fact, it would not be passed during the president's lifetime.

In August 1963, civil rights leader Martin Luther King Jr. waves to the vast crowds in Washington, D.C., after delivering his famous "I Have a Dream" speech.

Dallas

In November 1963, Jack and Jackie Kennedy went to Texas to confer with Texas Democratic leaders, hoping to bring an end to a nasty quarrel between factions. At 12:30 in the afternoon of November 22, while riding in a motorcade, the president was shot twice by a sniper. The president was rushed to Parkland Hospital in Dallas. After examining him, a doctor turned to Mrs. Kennedy and said, "Your husband has sustained a fatal wound."

Mrs. Kennedy nodded. "I know," she answered, her voice barely a whisper. A few minutes later, John Fitzgerald Kennedy died.

Mrs. Kennedy accompanied her husband's body back to *Air Force One*, the presidential plane that had brought them to Dallas. Vice President Lyndon B. Johnson, who had been in the presidential motorcade, was there to greet her. Inside the plane's cabin, with Mrs. Kennedy at his side, Johnson was sworn in as president to complete John F. Kennedy's term.

The young president's death shocked the world. People in many parts of the world wept when they heard the news. In London, bells of Westminster Abbey tolled without stopping for an hour, an honor that is usually reserved for members of Britain's royal family.

For two days, Kennedy's body lay in state, first in the White House and later in the Rotunda of the U.S. Capitol. Tens of thousands of people walked

Lyndon B. Johnson is sworn in as president onboard the presidential plane *Air Force One* after Kennedy's death on November 22, 1963. Johnson's wife, Lady Bird, is at the left and Jacqueline Kennedy is at the right.

slowly past his flag-draped coffin, paying their last respects. On November 25, his body was carried on a horse-drawn caisson (wagon) to St. Matthew's Cathedral for a funeral mass. A million people, many weeping, lined the route as

Kennedy family members leave the ceremony at the Capitol in Washington, D.C., where John F. Kennedy's body lies in state. They include his brother Robert Kennedy, his wife, Jacqueline, and his two young children, Caroline and John Jr.

the caisson passed. Millions watched on television. Then, as his family watched, the president was buried on a slope in Arlington National Cemetery, just outside of Washington. At the grave site, an eternal flame burns day and night.

The Aftermath

Soon after Kennedy's death, President Johnson appointed a seven-member commission, headed by Chief Justice Earl Warren, to investigate the assassination. The commission's report was published less than a year later, on September 27, 1964. It reported that that Lee Harvey Oswald, acting alone, fired the shots that killed the president. It found no evidence of a wider conspiracy. In spite of the report, doubters still believe that the assassination was a conspiracy pursued by foreign governments, by U.S. mobsters, or even by government agencies.

Lyndon Johnson also challenged Congress to pass the civil rights act as a tribute to the dead president. He used all his powers of persuasion to assure that Congress passed the bill without major changes. The following June, he signed the Civil Rights Act of 1964, which extended and strengthened the act of 1957 which he and Kennedy had worked to pass in the Senate. In 1965 Johnson helped pass the landmark Voting Rights Act, which allowed thousands of African Americans in the South to register and vote for the first time.

Robert Kennedy resigned as attorney general soon after his brother's death. In the fall of 1964, he was elected to the U.S. Senate from New York. When Lyndon Johnson announced in 1968 that he would not run for another term, Bobby Kennedy became a leading candidate, gaining broad support from Democratic voters seeking an end to the Vietnam War. On June 5, 1968, Kennedy won the California Democratic primary. Soon after his victory speech, however, he was shot and killed by an assassin.

John Kennedy's youngest brother, Ted, was elected to the U.S. Senate in 1962 to complete his brother's term. In 1969, Ted Kennedy's car ran off a bridge late one night. He narrowly escaped death, but his passenger, a young single woman on his staff, was drowned. This scandal ended his hopes of being elected to higher office, but Ted Kennedy remained in the U.S. Senate for more than 40 years, where he became a respected leader of his party.

Kennedy tragedies continued to the end of the 20th century. On July 16, 1999, Kennedy's only son, John Jr., was killed at the age of 38 when a plane he was piloting crashed into the Atlantic Ocean off the coast of Massachusetts. His wife and sister-in-law were also killed in the crash.

The Kennedy family's long string of tragedies and scandals caused many to suggest that there is a "Kennedy curse." Yet alongside the tragedies, the family also achieved a long history of constructive government service. It was the most influential political family in the land for more than 40 years.

The Kennedy Legacy ——————————————————

Like other presidents who died in office, Kennedy was long seen as a hero. His supporters celebrated his accomplishment and mourned the opportunities lost when he died so soon. Communities around the country named schools, streets, government buildings, and airports in his honor.

For many, Jack Kennedy and his family brought something special to the presidency. They were young and stylish in a way few earlier presidents had been. Jackie redecorated the White House, turning it into a showplace filled with fine art. Newspapers and magazines were filled with pictures of the young president, his wife, and their children. Caroline was six years old when her father died, and John F. Kennedy Jr., born a few days after Kennedy was elected president, was three.

Soon after the president's death, Jackie told an interviewer that his favorite music was from the Broadway musical *Camelot*, which is set in the court of the legendary King Arthur. She compared his presidency to the gathering of courtly knights in Camelot, but concluded sadly, "There will never be another Camelot."

President John F. Kennedy with his daughter Caroline on a summer cruise a few months before his death.

With the passage of time, Kennedy's reputation began to suffer. Historians pointed out that in nearly three years as president, he had not accomplished a great deal. Little important new legislation had been passed. In foreign affairs, he took responsibility for the disastrous Bay of Pigs invasion and handled the Cuban missile crisis with courage and skill, but his only major initiative was the agreement with other nuclear powers to limit dangerous nuclear testing.

Researchers dug into Kennedy's private life. Breathless books reported on his affairs with other women, on the frightening state of his health, and on his use of powerful drugs that may have weakened his judgment. Others reported on the role his family's money and his father's political influence played in his career, seeming to reduce his importance as an individual.

Even so, many people still see John F. Kennedy's presidency as a shining moment. Dogged by tragedy, illness, and pain, Kennedy spoke confidently of a better future. He urged his country to believe in its most cherished ideals and to work together to make these ideals a reality. He was willing to use the powers of government to protect and help its citizens, but he realized the power of citizens themselves to do great things. "Ask not what your country can do for you," he urged, "ask what you can do for your country."

Fast Facts | John Fitzgerald Kennedy

Birth:	May 29, 1917
Birthplace:	Brookline, Massachusetts
Parents:	Joseph Patrick Kennedy and Rose Fitzgerald Kennedy
Brothers & Sisters:	Joseph Jr. (Joe) (1915–1944)
	Rosemary (1918–)
	Kathleen (1920–1948)
	Eunice (1921–)
	Patricia (1924–)
	Robert (Bobby) (1925–1968)
	Jean (1928–)
	Edward (Ted) (1932–)
Education:	Harvard College, graduated 1940
Occupation:	Author, legislator
Marriage:	To Jacqueline Lee Bouvier, September 12, 1953
Children:	(see First Lady Fast Facts, next page)
Political Party:	Democratic
Public Offices:	1947–1953 U.S. Congressman from Massachusetts
	1953–1961 U.S. Senator from Massachusetts
	1961–1963 President of the United States
His Vice President:	Lyndon Baines Johnson
Major Actions as President:	1961 Created the Peace Corps, backed Cuban Bay of Pigs invasion
	1962 Achieved peaceful solution in Cuban missile crisis
	1963 Signed Nuclear Test Ban Treaty with Soviet Union, Great Britain
Death:	November 22, 1963 in Dallas, Texas
Age at Death:	46 years
Burial Place:	Arlington National Cemetery, Arlington, Virginia

Fast Facts

Jacqueline (Jackie) Bouvier Kennedy

Birth:	July 28, 1929
Birthplace:	Southampton, New York
Parents:	John Vernon Bouvier III and Janet Lee Bouvier
Sister:	Caroline Lee Bouvier (later Princess Lee Radziwill) (1933–)
Education:	Vassar College; the Sorbonne (Paris, France); George Washington University, graduated 1951
Marriage:	To John Fitzgerald Kennedy, September 12, 1953
	To Aristotle Onassis, 1968
Children:	Caroline (1957–)
	John Fitzgerald Jr. (1960–1999)
Died:	May 19, 1994
Age at Death:	64 years
Burial Place:	Arlington National Cemetery, Arlington, Virginia

Timeline

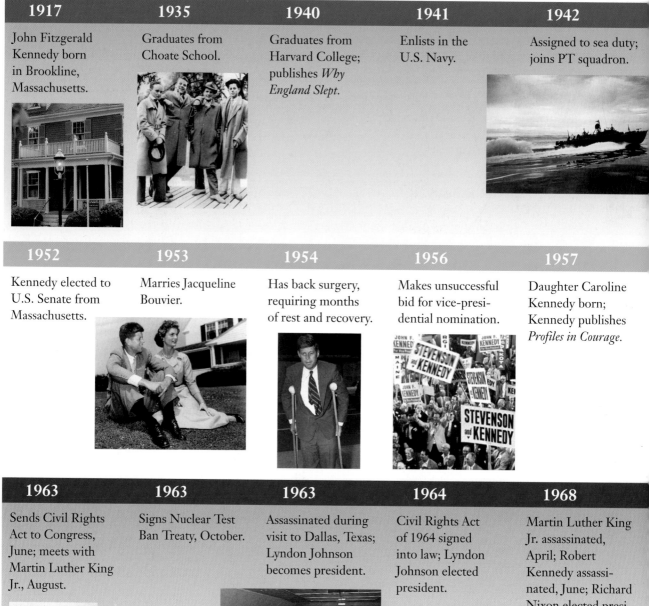

1917	1935	1940	1941	1942
John Fitzgerald Kennedy born in Brookline, Massachusetts.	Graduates from Choate School.	Graduates from Harvard College; publishes *Why England Slept*.	Enlists in the U.S. Navy.	Assigned to sea duty; joins PT squadron.

1952	1953	1954	1956	1957
Kennedy elected to U.S. Senate from Massachusetts.	Marries Jacqueline Bouvier.	Has back surgery, requiring months of rest and recovery.	Makes unsuccessful bid for vice-presidential nomination.	Daughter Caroline Kennedy born; Kennedy publishes *Profiles in Courage*.

1963	1963	1963	1964	1968
Sends Civil Rights Act to Congress, June; meets with Martin Luther King Jr., August.	Signs Nuclear Test Ban Treaty, October.	Assassinated during visit to Dallas, Texas; Lyndon Johnson becomes president.	Civil Rights Act of 1964 signed into law; Lyndon Johnson elected president.	Martin Luther King Jr. assassinated, April; Robert Kennedy assassinated, June; Richard Nixon elected president, November.

1943	1944	1945	1946	1948
Enters combat in the South Pacific; *PT-109* is sunk, Kennedy rescues crew.	Kennedy's older brother, Joe Jr., killed in action in Europe.	Kennedy discharged from U.S. Navy.	Elected to U.S. Congress from Massachusetts 11th district; re-elected 1948 and 1950.	Kennedy's sister Kathleen killed in plane crash in France.

1958	1960	1960	1961	1962
Elected to second term in U.S. Senate.	Wins Democratic nomination for president, July; defeats Republican Richard Nixon for the presidency, November.	Son John Fitzgerald Kennedy Jr. born.	Appoints brother Robert Kennedy attorney general; creates Peace Corps; backs ill-fated invasion of Cuba at the Bay of Pigs.	Demands that Soviets remove missiles from Cuba, orders blockade; crisis ended by negotiation.

Glossary

belligerent: warlike

boycott: refusal by a group to buy goods or services from a business until objectionable rules or laws are changed

cabinet: in U.S. government, the heads of major federal departments who act as senior advisers to the president

censure: condemnation or severe criticism by an official body

civil rights: rights under law to be treated equally with other citizens

clandestine: secret

counsel: legal adviser

drafted: called for induction into military service

ensign: the lowest officer rank in the U.S. Navy

isolationist: a person who favors avoiding alliances with foreign governments and involvement in foreign wars

page: a young person who serves as an assistant to an officeholder, delivering messages and running errands; congressional pages provide such services for U.S. representatives

primary election: an election in which members of a political party vote for candidates to run as party nominees in a general election

quarantine: actions prohibiting a ship from entering a harbor because it may carry disease or dangerous cargo; a blockade

recession: an economic slowdown; a mild depression

refugee: a person who leaves a country because of personal danger or political persecution

segregated: kept separate from others in a society by the force of law

Further Reading

★ ★ ★ ★ ★

Darraj, Susan. *John F. Kennedy*. Broomall, PA: Chelsea House, 2004.

Rivera, Sheila. *The Assassination of John F. Kennedy*. Minneapolis, MN: Abdo Publishing, 2004.

Spies, Karen. *John F. Kennedy*. Springfield, NJ: Enslow Publishers, 1997.

MORE ADVANCED READING

Dallek, Robert. *An Unfinished Life*. New York: Little Brown and Company, 2003.

Goodwin, Doris Kearns. *The Fitzgeralds and the Kennedys*. New York: Simon and Schuster, 1987.

Leamer, Lawrence. *The Kennedy Men*. New York: William Morrow, 2001.

Places to Visit

John F. Kennedy Library and Museum
Columbia Point
Boston, MA 02125-3398
1-866-JFK-1960 or (617) 514-1600
www.jfklibrary.org

The museum portrays the life, leadership, and legacy of President Kennedy, conveys his enthusiasm for politics and public service, and illustrates the nature of the office of president. The library houses John F. Kennedy's personal papers and other documents of value to researchers and historians.

**Graves of John F. Kennedy and
Jacqueline Kennedy**
Arlington National Cemetery
Arlington, VA

Kennedy is only the second president to be interred in Arlington. The other is William Howard Taft. Kennedy's grave and the eternal flame memorial lighted on the day of his burial are visited by thousands of people each year. On May 23, 1994, Jacqueline Kennedy Onassis was buried next to President Kennedy. The only other first lady buried in Arlington is Helen Taft, William Howard Taft's wife.

The White House
1600 Pennsylvania Avenue NW
Washington, DC 20500
Visitors' Info Line: (202) 456-7041

John and Jacqueline Kennedy lived here from 1961 until his death in 1963.

Online Sites of Interest

★ **Internet Public Library, Presidents of the United States (IPL POTUS)**

http://www.potus.com/jfkennedy.html

Includes concise information about Kennedy and his presidency and provides links to other sites of interest.

★ **American President.org**

www.americanpresident.org/history/

Offers information about American presidents and the presidency, including biographies of Kennedy and all other presidents.

★ **Grolier**

http://gi.grolier.com/presidents/

This site, sponsored by the publisher of reference material, offers links leading to information about all the presidents. Material includes brief biographies at different reading levels, presidential portraits, and presidential election results.

★ **Kennedy's Health Problems**

www.pbs.org/wgbh/amex/kennedys/sfeature/sf_dallek.html#a

This site offers a discussion of Kennedy's health by Robert Dallek, presidential historian and author.

www.doctorzebra.com/prez

★ **The White House**

www.whitehouse.gov/history/presidents

Offers brief biographical articles on each president and first lady.

★ **The John F. Kennedy Library and Museum**

www.jfklibrary.org

Offers information about hours of operation, displays, and research materials.

Table of Presidents

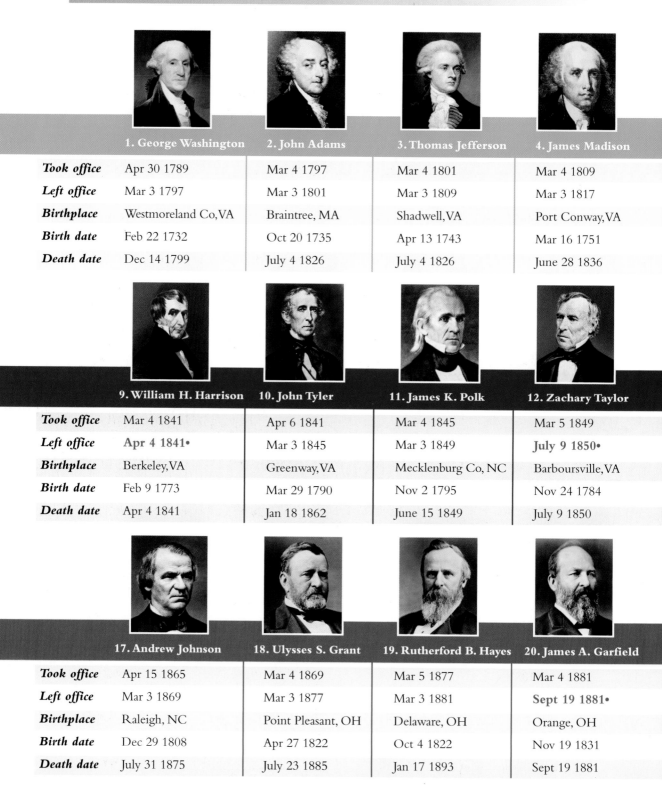

	1. George Washington	2. John Adams	3. Thomas Jefferson	4. James Madison
Took office	Apr 30 1789	Mar 4 1797	Mar 4 1801	Mar 4 1809
Left office	Mar 3 1797	Mar 3 1801	Mar 3 1809	Mar 3 1817
Birthplace	Westmoreland Co, VA	Braintree, MA	Shadwell, VA	Port Conway, VA
Birth date	Feb 22 1732	Oct 20 1735	Apr 13 1743	Mar 16 1751
Death date	Dec 14 1799	July 4 1826	July 4 1826	June 28 1836

	9. William H. Harrison	10. John Tyler	11. James K. Polk	12. Zachary Taylor
Took office	Mar 4 1841	Apr 6 1841	Mar 4 1845	Mar 5 1849
Left office	Apr 4 1841•	Mar 3 1845	Mar 3 1849	July 9 1850•
Birthplace	Berkeley, VA	Greenway, VA	Mecklenburg Co, NC	Barboursville, VA
Birth date	Feb 9 1773	Mar 29 1790	Nov 2 1795	Nov 24 1784
Death date	Apr 4 1841	Jan 18 1862	June 15 1849	July 9 1850

	17. Andrew Johnson	18. Ulysses S. Grant	19. Rutherford B. Hayes	20. James A. Garfield
Took office	Apr 15 1865	Mar 4 1869	Mar 5 1877	Mar 4 1881
Left office	Mar 3 1869	Mar 3 1877	Mar 3 1881	Sept 19 1881•
Birthplace	Raleigh, NC	Point Pleasant, OH	Delaware, OH	Orange, OH
Birth date	Dec 29 1808	Apr 27 1822	Oct 4 1822	Nov 19 1831
Death date	July 31 1875	July 23 1885	Jan 17 1893	Sept 19 1881

5. James Monroe	6. John Quincy Adams	7. Andrew Jackson	8. Martin Van Buren
Mar 4 1817	Mar 4 1825	Mar 4 1829	Mar 4 1837
Mar 3 1825	Mar 3 1829	Mar 3 1837	Mar 3 1841
Westmoreland Co, VA	Braintree, MA	The Waxhaws, SC	Kinderhook, NY
Apr 28 1758	July 11 1767	Mar 15 1767	Dec 5 1782
July 4 1831	Feb 23 1848	June 8 1845	July 24 1862

13. Millard Fillmore	14. Franklin Pierce	15. James Buchanan	16. Abraham Lincoln
July 9 1850	Mar 4 1853	Mar 4 1857	Mar 4 1861
Mar 3 1853	Mar 3 1857	Mar 3 1861	Apr 15 1865•
Locke Township, NY	Hillsborough, NH	Cove Gap, PA	Hardin Co, KY
Jan 7 1800	Nov 23 1804	Apr 23 1791	Feb 12 1809
Mar 8 1874	Oct 8 1869	June 1 1868	Apr 15 1865

21. Chester A. Arthur	22. Grover Cleveland	23. Benjamin Harrison	24. Grover Cleveland
Sept 19 1881	Mar 4 1885	Mar 4 1889	Mar 4 1893
Mar 3 1885	Mar 3 1889	Mar 3 1893	Mar 3 1897
Fairfield, VT	Caldwell, NJ	North Bend, OH	Caldwell, NJ
Oct 5 1829	Mar 18 1837	Aug 20 1833	Mar 18 1837
Nov 18 1886	June 24 1908	Mar 13 1901	June 24 1908

25. William McKinley

Took office	Mar 4 1897
Left office	Sept 14 1901•
Birthplace	Niles, OH
Birth date	Jan 29 1843
Death date	Sept 14 1901

26. Theodore Roosevelt

Took office	Sept 14 1901
Left office	Mar 3 1909
Birthplace	New York, NY
Birth date	Oct 27 1858
Death date	Jan 6 1919

27. William H. Taft

Took office	Mar 4 1909
Left office	Mar 3 1913
Birthplace	Cincinnati, OH
Birth date	Sept 15 1857
Death date	Mar 8 1930

28. Woodrow Wilson

Took office	Mar 4 1913
Left office	Mar 3 1921
Birthplace	Staunton, VA
Birth date	Dec 28 1856
Death date	Feb 3 1924

33. Harry S. Truman

Took office	Apr 12 1945
Left office	Jan 20 1953
Birthplace	Lamar, MO
Birth date	May 8 1884
Death date	Dec 26 1972

34. Dwight D. Eisenhower

Took office	Jan 20 1953
Left office	Jan 20 1961
Birthplace	Denison, TX
Birth date	Oct 14 1890
Death date	Mar 28 1969

35. John F. Kennedy

Took office	Jan 20 1961
Left office	Nov 22 1963•
Birthplace	Brookline, MA
Birth date	May 29 1917
Death date	Nov 22 1963

36. Lyndon B. Johnson

Took office	Nov 22 1963
Left office	Jan 20 1969
Birthplace	Johnson City, TX
Birth date	Aug 27 1908
Death date	Jan 22 1973

41. George Bush

Took office	Jan 20 1989
Left office	Jan 20 1993
Birthplace	Milton, MA
Birth date	June 12 1924
Death date	——

42. Bill Clinton

Took office	Jan 20 1993
Left office	Jan 20 2001
Birthplace	Hope, AR
Birth date	Aug 19 1946
Death date	——

43. George W. Bush

Took office	Jan 20 2001
Left office	——
Birthplace	New Haven, CT
Birth date	July 6 1946

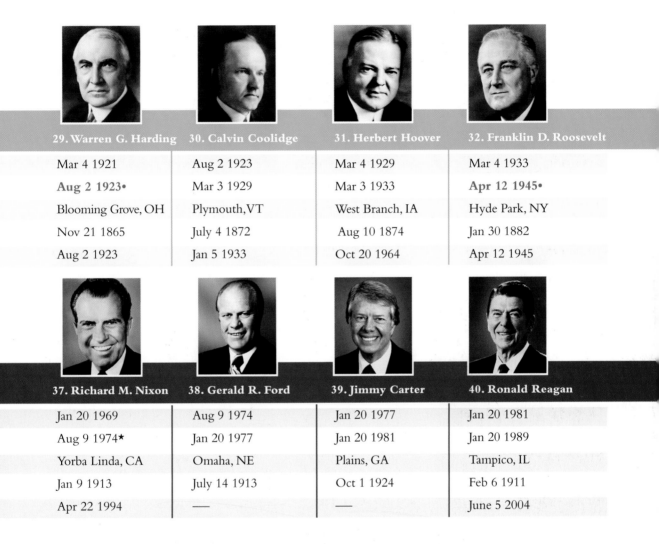

29. Warren G. Harding	30. Calvin Coolidge	31. Herbert Hoover	32. Franklin D. Roosevelt
Mar 4 1921	Aug 2 1923	Mar 4 1929	Mar 4 1933
Aug 2 1923•	Mar 3 1929	Mar 3 1933	Apr 12 1945•
Blooming Grove, OH	Plymouth, VT	West Branch, IA	Hyde Park, NY
Nov 21 1865	July 4 1872	Aug 10 1874	Jan 30 1882
Aug 2 1923	Jan 5 1933	Oct 20 1964	Apr 12 1945

37. Richard M. Nixon	38. Gerald R. Ford	39. Jimmy Carter	40. Ronald Reagan
Jan 20 1969	Aug 9 1974	Jan 20 1977	Jan 20 1981
Aug 9 1974★	Jan 20 1977	Jan 20 1981	Jan 20 1989
Yorba Linda, CA	Omaha, NE	Plains, GA	Tampico, IL
Jan 9 1913	July 14 1913	Oct 1 1924	Feb 6 1911
Apr 22 1994	—	—	June 5 2004

• Indicates the president died while in office.

★ Richard Nixon resigned before his term expired.

Index

About the Author

Kieran Doherty is the award-winning author of 14 books for young readers. A career journalist and magazine writer before turning his attention to writing for children and teens, he particularly enjoys writing historical nonfiction. Doherty, an avid sailor, lives in Lake Worth, Florida, with his wife, Lynne.